My Sister Is Sick...

What About Me?

Written by Mary Kay & Eli Olson

Illustrated by Becky Wosick

This book is dedicated to my mom and dad. Without you, this book would have never come to be. And to my husband, Brad, and kids, Eli and Ella: thank you for always believing in me. How lucky am I to spend this life with you.

—Mary Kay Olson

This book is dedicated to my mom, dad and Ella. Thank you guys for being caring and understanding that this is a lot to go through. Also, to my counselor Ben Monseth. Thank you for teaching me how to handle my ADHD and controlling my feelings.

—Eli Olson

Look for the cardinal on each page
as it lovingly follows Eli throughout his story.

Blue 42!
Blue 42!
Hut-Hut HIKE!

Hello, team! My name is Eli and I am ten years old. I'm pretty much a normal kid. I like playing with friends, going on adventures, playing games, and I LOVE football.

I mean REALLY love football.

I also love my family.

But there is something big going on in my family that I need to talk to you about.

I have a sister who gets sick. A lot.

She is eight years old and her name is Ella. She was born with many health problems.

If I tell you everything she has gone through, you would not believe it.

Her list is SOOOOO long and very complicated.

If you had to read the whole thing, you would probably get really confused, stop reading this book and throw it out the window.

Don't do that.

Your parent paid good money for this book.

I will, however, tell you the big things on
Ella's list:

She has had nine surgeries since she has
been born (one was in a different state).

She has had a hundred icky tests. Okay,
maybe it's not a hundred, but I'm sure it
feels that way to her.

She has had many IV's. If you've never heard of an IV, be thankful. She has had to take different medicines. Lots of medicine.

She goes to countless
doctor appointments.

Is countless a number?

She has to do a long medical procedure
every day when she is at home.

She hates it.

My aunt even made a song about it. If
I sang it to you, you would never be
able to get it out of your head.

Ever.

Ella has had to be **VERY brave** and **VERY strong.**

This has not been easy on her. But it hasn't been easy on me either.

I haven't had to do the things on Ella's list, but I've had my own stuff.

This might surprise you, but I have a list too. My list
is very different than Ella's.

It is made up of big feelings that scare me sometimes.
My list is hard to talk about, but I promise you one
thing, it is the truth.

My truth.

The first thing on my list is WORRY.
When Ella goes in for surgery I worry about her and if she is going to be okay. If I worry too much my stomach hurts and feels really sick.

I worry about my mom and dad too.

Especially my mom.

She cries sometimes and that makes me sad. I want to help her but don't Know how.
Most times I will go and hug her.

She likes that.

The next thing on my list is ANGER.
Say that with me.
ANGER!!!
Ok, make an angry face!
Stop it!
You're making me laugh!

I am angry about many things. Angry that Ella gets so much attention for being sick and I'm not getting enough attention.

I am angry when people ask how Ella is doing and not how I am doing.

I am angry that the focus is always on her and I am forgotten. Well, maybe not forgotten, but sometimes it feels that way.

I am angry that Ella has to do a procedure every day and sometimes we have to miss fun things because of it.

Ok, one more angry face.

Third on my list is **SADNESS.**

Seeing my sister sick makes me really sad. Especially when she is in pain.

I want to help her but can't.

I get sad when my mom and dad have to sleep at the hospital with Ella. One time they even had to fly on a plane to another hospital and were gone for what seemed like forever.

I was with my grandma and papa and aunt and uncle, but it was still really hard on me.

I get sad when people say, "We are praying for Ella," and they don't say they are praying for me too.

I know they aren't doing it on purpose, but it hurts my feelings.

People send packages and cards to Ella and not to me. I know she's the
one that's sick, but remember this isn't easy on me either.
I just don't want people to forget about me.

Well, those are the top three things on my list.

Whew. I'm tired.
Let's stop for a water break.

Just kidding. I know this is just a book.

Maybe you have a brother or sister that is sick. If you do, I want you to know that you are not alone.

I want to help you.

But, in order for me to do that we need a game plan.

A SERIOUS game plan!

Ok. Here we go!
We need to huddle up because what I am about to tell you is
REEEAAAALLLLLYYYY important.

ALL FEELINGS ARE OKAY. Say that with me,

"ALL FEELINGS ARE OKAY."

I'm serious.

Every single feeling is okay. Don't ever feel bad about something you are feeling. It's what we do with those feelings that matters most.

OK? Understood?
Alright, then! Hands in! Feelings on three! One, two, three,

FEELINGS!

ELI'S GAME PLAN #1: Don't hide your feelings

The worst thing you can do is stuff your feelings in your belly like a burrito. You will feel sick.
I know it's hard, but you need to share your feelings with someone you trust. People won't know how you are feeling unless you tell them.

Here's an example of what I would say: "I felt sad today when Ella got two cards in the mail and I didn't get any. It makes me feel like people don't care about me."

See? That wasn't hard!

BOOM! Chest bump!

Wait. Don't do that.

#2: Have a plan when you have big feelings

Cool-down spot:
I have a special place in my house where I can go and cool down. My spot is in the family room next to the couch. I have a bean bag chair, some favorite books, pictures and toys that I love.

Where could your cool-down spot be? Maybe your room, or somewhere where you feel safe.

Take Belly Breaths: In through your nose and out through your mouth. And go slow. Try not to breathe too fast.

Move your body! Do jumping jacks, sit ups or run in place to get your frustration out. You could even do a silly dance!

This may sound weird, but you have to tell yourself positive things. For example, I might say,

Or my favorite: "I'm just downright awesome!"
Smile big and believe it!

Oooooohhhh man, it feels good to talk about this!

REALLY GOOD!

Can we just stop and do a

touchdown dance?

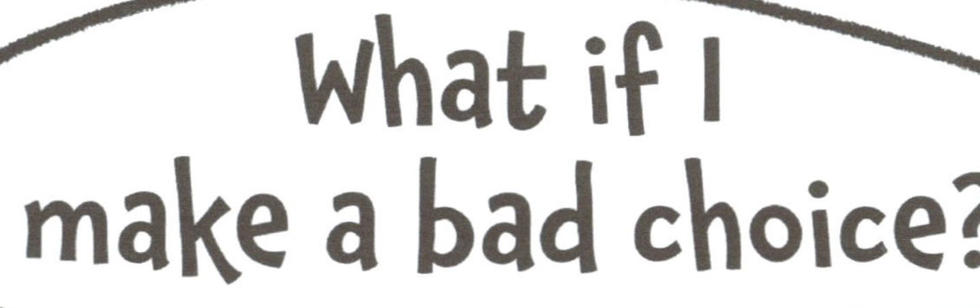

Wait a minute people, it looks like we have a question from the crowd. Go ahead, friend.

**Whoa.
TIME OUT
FOLKS!!!**

We have a very
serious question.
We need to take
a knee for
this one.

Friends, you need to know that it's okay to make mistakes.

Seriously.

Everyone, and I mean **EVERYONE** makes mistakes.
We just need to own what we did and apologize.

How do you "own it"?

Say you're sorry. And not just "Sorry" with your eyes down.

Look at the person and say, "I'm sorry for _______. I won't do that again."

It's never easy to apologize, but you will feel so much better after you do.

Well, there's the game plan!

It has really helped me and I hope it will help you too.

Always remember...

You are BRAVE. You are STRONG. Many people LOVE you.
Keep using your WORDS. I KNOW you can do this!

And don't forget to BREATHE! In through your nose and out through your mouth.

(Warning: Don't do this while eating.)

Your friend, Eli
(resume touchdown dance)

About the Authors

Mary Kay Olson is a speaker, educator and author of "My Sister is Sick, What About Me?" With over two decades teaching elementary education, Mary Kay has a unique take on how to talk to kids with emotional struggles. Mary Kay's accomplishments range from appearing on the Oprah Winfrey episode of the documentary, "Dear..." on AppleTV+, being CEO of her nonprofit organization, "Praise Up", and traveling the country speaking to different groups on how to find hope after a traumatic event. Mary Kay lives in Rogers, MN with her husband, Brad, and two kids, Eli and Ella, and their sweet dog, Maui. Visit Mary Kay at www.praiseup.org, or email her at maryKay.olson@praiseup.org to schedule a speaking engagement.

Eli Olson is a student at Rogers High School and author of "My Sister is Sick, What About Me?" Eli has lived this story and has an amazing way to talk to others about his life experiences. His passion is playing tennis, being on his high school's eSports Team for Rocket League and playing soccer. He lives in Rogers, MN with his mom and dad, his sister, Ella, and his dog, Maui. His life goal is to be a counselor and help other kids manage their emotions.

About the Illustrator

From a young age Becky loved to draw, paint and think creatively. This passion led her to a career in the architecture field designing entertainment and hospitality spaces. Illustrating children's books has been one of Becky's lifelong dreams. Helping children through the illustrations of "My Sister is Sick, What About Me?" means a lot to her. Becky lives in Minnesota with her husband and 3 young children. When she isn't creating, Becky enjoys spending time with her family, being outdoors and reading.

About Atmosphere Press

Atmosphere Press is an independent, full-service publisher for excellent books in all genres and for all audiences. Learn more about what we do at atmospherepress.com.

We encourage you to check out some of Atmosphere's latest releases, which are available at Amazon.com and via order from your local bookstore:

Bella the Scientist Goes to Outer Space, by Silvana Spence and Isabella Spence

Tossing Stars, by Tanya Sousa

A Boy and His Bones, by Michael Johnson

Super STEM, by Lauren Yu

L.E. Ant, by Michael Hedman

Jenny Bear: A Journey Towards Healthy Grieving, by Caleb Potter

Rooster Wrangling, by Tracey Willet

Happy Trails Camper Stories: Lucy Learns to Share, by Sharlene Novak

My New Human, by Kelsey Summer

Night Stallion, by Martha White

Nami's New Friend, by Mandy Namjou Yorn

The Super Guide to Becoming a Superhero, by Michael DeLorenzo

A to Z and Covid 19, by Barrie Berson Frankel

Wildly Perfect, by Brooke McMahan

Do Lions Cry?, by Erina White

Sadie and Charley Finding Their Way, by Bonnie Griesemer